A DIFFERENT LIGHT

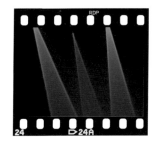

Lewis Lee Photography

VARI*LITE®
The Automated Lighting Company

ISBN 0-9658800-0-1

Design of 'A Different Light' is by
Pritchards Creative Communications Limited
Gratton House, Gratton Street, Cheltenham, Gloucestershire GL50 2AS, England.

We at Vari-Lite extend our deep gratitude to everyone at Pritchards
for their invaluable contribution of time, effort and creativity
in the publication of this book.

Published by Vari-Lite, Inc.
Dallas, Texas, USA.

Printed in Singapore.

This book is dedicated to the life and and work of

Kirby Kennedy Wyatt II
1943 - 1995

With his unique blend of creative abilities, Kirby's contribution to all
of the Vari-Lite companies and to the entertainment industry are of
great and lasting value.

Kirby's legacy to us is his unique insight. In a world of people
who commonly tell us what we want to hear, Kirby told us
what we needed to hear - the truth.

We could ask for no better friend and colleague.
We miss him deeply.

Profits from this special book will be donated to
DIFFA: The Design Industries Foundation Fighting Aids
and *Broadway Cares.*

DIFFA's selection reflects Kirby's active participation in DIFFA events.
Broadway Cares was chosen because Kirby was first and foremost a theatre person.

▲ Artist: *Genesis* Lighting Designer: *Alan Owen* Year: *1983*

Foreword

By Genesis

Preserving the true sound of a live concert in a recording is the ultimate goal of every sound engineer. In a similar way, every photographer strives to capture the dynamism and atmosphere of each event he or she shoots.

Lewis Lee is the only photographer we know who can create this elusive picture to such a consistently high standard.

Lewis's photography illustrates not just the set, the lighting or the performers; it captures the whole performance in every detail. Rather than simply freezing brief frames of action, a Lewis Lee picture allows you to enjoy the whole spectacle, just as if you are in the audience, on the night itself.

Those that have been captivated by the magic of a live music concert or mesmerized by the power of theater, will understand the significance of this unique collection.

As performers, we know that everyone who walks onto a stage has one recurring question in the back of their mind: how does the show look from the other side of the footlights?

Lewis Lee's work provides the answer with warmth and integrity.

Tony Banks

Phil Collins

Mike Rutherford

Tony Smith

▲ Artist: *The Cure* Lighting Designer: *LeRoy Bennett* Year: *1992*

Introduction

By Rusty Brutsché

Jim Clark, Jack Maxson and I founded Vari-Lite in 1981 with the help of Tony Smith and Genesis. Vari-Lite grew out of Showco, a company Jack and I started in a garage in 1970. We built Showco and Vari-Lite with the dreams and talents of many creative people. Sharing a passion for the world of entertainment and performing arts, they became not only our colleagues, but our friends. Each was driven by a desire to explore new techniques and technologies to create outstanding shows. This book features the work of one of our most talented and respected friends. It is presented as a tribute to another friend who is sadly no longer with us.

When Lewis Lee decided to combine his love of live music with his fascination for photography, it became clear to those around him that Lewis has a special gift. This extraordinary selection of Lewis' pictures chronicles some of the many memorable moments in Vari-Lite's history.

This collection of photographs also serves as a public acknowledgement of our fond memories of Kirby Wyatt. Kirby played an integral part in the many successes of Showco and helped to lay the foundation for Vari-Lite. His death was a tremendous loss to his family, his friends and the entertainment industry to which he contributed so much warmth, vision and innovation.

We would like to thank the performers, designers, managers, road crews, all of the lighting companies, and all of the other participants who have brought about these many events. They have made this book possible.

There could not be a more appropriate way to remember Kirby than through this unique record of entertainment lighting.

Rusty Brutsché
President and CEO
Vari-Lite International, Inc.

▲ Artist: *Kenny G* Lighting Designer: *Val Groth* Year: *1993*

▲ Artist: *Dio* Lighting Designer: *Paul Dexter* Year: *1985*

▲ Artist: *Bryan Adams* Lighting Designers: *LeRoy Bennett, John Featherstone* Year: *1992*
◀ Artist: *Depeche Mode* Lighting Designer: *Jane Spiers* Year: *1987*

Artist: *The Pretenders* Lighting Designer: *Chas Herington* Year: *1987* ▲
Artist: *David Bowie* Lighting Designer: *Allen Branton* Year: *1987* ▶

▲ Artist: *Lorrie Morgan* Lighting Designer: *Seth Jackson* Year: *1996*

◀ Artist: *The Rolling Stones* Lighting Designer: *Patrick Woodroffe* Year: *1994*

▲ Artist: *Siegfried & Roy* Designer: *Andrew Bridge* Year: *1990* (Courtesy of Feld Entertainment)

▲ Artist: *Jesus Jones* Lighting Designer: *Simon Sidi* Year: *1993*

Event: *The 39th GRAMMY® Awards* Lighting Designer: *Bob Dickinson* Year: *1996* ▲
Artist: *Don Henley* Lighting Designer: *Steve Cohen* Year: *1991* ▶

▲ Artist: *Genesis* Lighting Designer: *Alan Owen* Year: *1983*
◀ Artist: *Genesis* Lighting Designer: *Alan Owen* Year: *1987*

Artist: *Genesis* Lighting Designer: *Alan Owen* Year: *1987* ▲
Artist: *Genesis* Lighting Designer: *Alan Owen* Year: *1983* ▶

▲ Artist: *Sade* Lighting Designer: *LeRoy Bennett* Year: *1993*

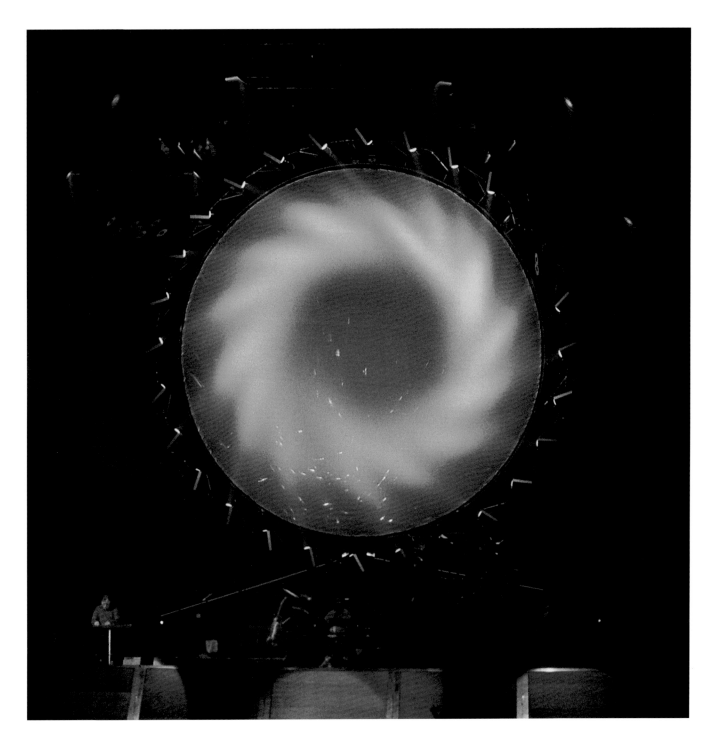

▲ Artist: *Pink Floyd* Lighting Designer: *Marc Brickman* Year: *1994*

Artist: *Pink Floyd* Lighting Designer: *Marc Brickman* Year: *1987* ▲
Artist: *George Michael* Lighting Designer: *LeRoy Bennett* Year: *1991* ▶

▲ Artist: *Billy Idol* Lighting Designer: *Steve Cohen* Year: *1987*

◀ Artist: *Genesis* Lighting Designer: *Alan Owen* Year: *1983*

Artist: *Michael W Smith* Lighting Designer: *James Taylor* Year: *1993* ▲
Artist: *Depeche Mode* Lighting Designer: *LeRoy Bennett* Year: *1993* ▶

▲ Artist: *Genesis* Lighting Designer: *Alan Owen* Year: *1983*

◀ Artist: *Depeche Mode* Lighting Designer: *Jane Spiers* Year: *1987*

Artist: *Billy Joel & Elton John* Lighting Designer: *Steve Cohen* Year: *1994* ▲
Artist: *The Cure* Lighting Designer: *LeRoy Bennett* Year: *1992* ▶

▲ Artist: *The Cure* Lighting Designer: *LeRoy Bennett* Year: *1992*
◀ Artist: *The Rolling Stones* Lighting Designer: *Patrick Woodroffe* Year: *1994*

Artist: *The Tempest* Lighting Designer: *Sumio Yoshii* Year: *1996* ▲
Artist: *Jesus Jones* Lighting Designer: *Simon Sidi* Year: *1993* ▶

▲ Artist: *Yanni* Lighting Designer: *David 'Gurn' Kaniski* Year: *1993*
◀ Artist: *David Bowie* Lighting Designer: *Allen Branton* Year: *1987*

Artist: *The Cure* Lighting Designer: *LeRoy Bennett* Year: *1992* ▲
Artist: *Genesis* Lighting Designer: *Marc Brickman* Year: *1992* ▶

▲ Artist: *Mötley Crüe* Lighting Designer: *Manfred 'Ollie' Olma* Year: *1990*

◀ Artist: *David Bowie* Lighting Designer: *Allen Branton* Year: *1983*

▲ Event: *The 39th GRAMMY® Awards* Lighting Designer: *Bob Dickinson* Year: *1996*

▲ Artist: *Paul McCartney* Lighting Designer: *Marc Brickman* Year: *1993*

▲ Artist: *BRING IN 'DA NOISE, BRING IN 'DA FUNK* Lighting Designers: *Jules Fisher, Peggy Eisenhauer* Year: *1996*

◀ Artist: *Billy Joel & Elton John* Lighting Designer: *Steve Cohen* Year: *1995*

Artist: *Def Leppard* Year: *1993* ▲

Artist: *The Rolling Stones* Lighting Designer: *Patrick Woodroffe* Year: *1989* ▶

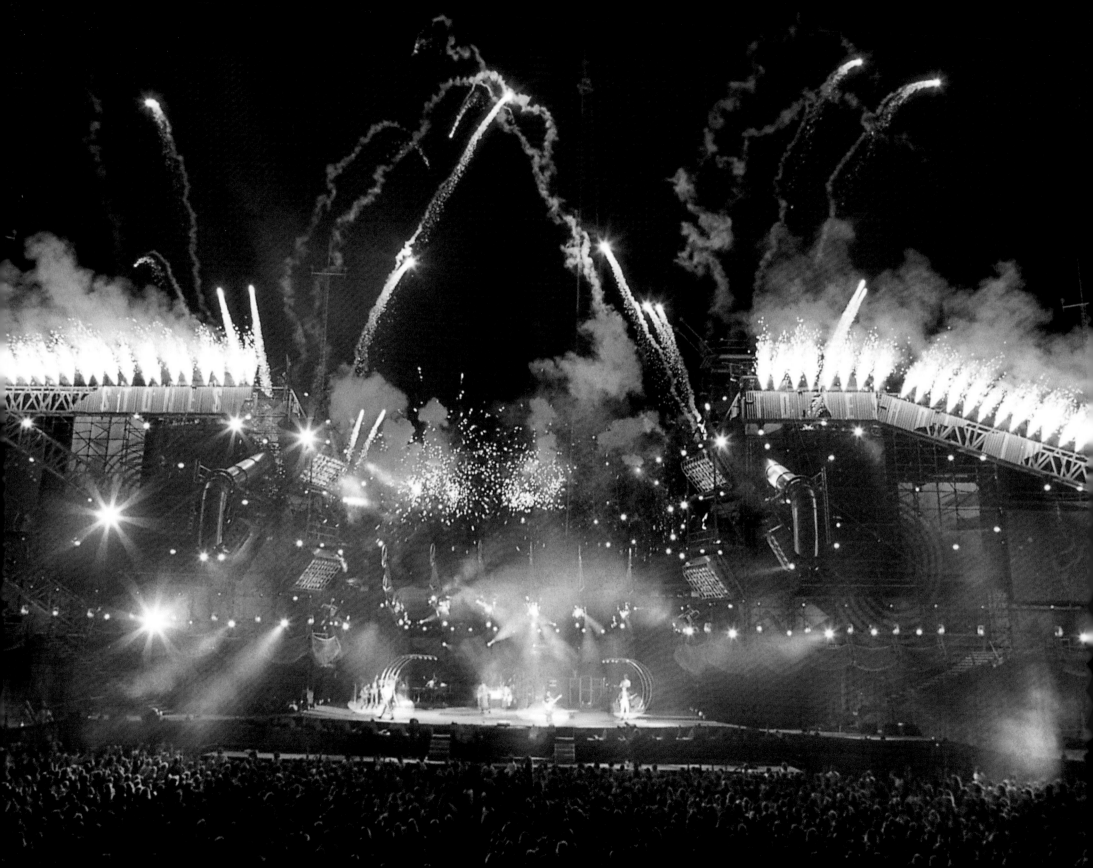

▲ Artist: *Moody Blues* Lighting Designer: *Michael Keller* Year: *1991*

◀ Artist: *BRING IN 'DA NOISE, BRING IN 'DA FUNK* Lighting Designers: *Jules Fisher, Peggy Eisenhauer* Year: *1996*

▲ Artist: *Lorrie Morgan* Lighting Designer: *Seth Jackson* Year: *1995*

▲ Artist: *Mary Chapin Carpenter* Lighting Designer: *Allen Branton* Year: *1995*

Artist: *BRING IN 'DA NOISE, BRING IN 'DA FUNK* Lighting Designers: *Jules Fisher, Peggy Eisenhauer* Year: *1996* ▲

Artist: *Spin Doctors* Lighting Designer: *Jimmy Pettinato* Year: *1994* ▶

▲ Artist: *Billy Joel & Elton John* Lighting Designer: *Steve Cohen* Year: *1994*

◀ Artist: *Jesus Jones* Lighting Designer: *Simon Sidi* Year: *1993*

Artist: *Phil Collins* Lighting Designer: *Patrick Woodroffe* Year: *1994* ▲
Artist: *New Order* Lighting Designer: *Andy Liddle* Year: *1989* ▶

▲ Artist: *Genesis* Lighting Designer: *Alan Owen* Year: *1987*

▲ Artist: *Genesis* Lighting Designer: *Alan Owen* Year: *1987*

▲ Artist: *The Cure* Lighting Designer: *LeRoy Bennett* Year: *1996*

▲ Artist: *Phil Collins* Year: *1990*

Artist: *Genesis* Lighting Designer: *Alan Owen* Year: *1987* ▲
Artist: *Psychedelic Furs* Lighting Designer: *Alec Nisic* Year: *1990* ▶

▲ Artist: *Bette Midler* Lighting Designer: *Peter Morse* Year: *1994*

▲ Artist: *Don Henley* Lighting Designer: *Steve Cohen* Year: *1989*

Artist: *Pink Floyd* Lighting Designer: *Marc Brickman* Year: *1987* ▲
Artist: *The Rolling Stones* Lighting Designer: *Patrick Woodroffe* Year: *1994* ▶

▲ Artist: *George Michael* Lighting Designer: *LeRoy Bennett* Year: *1991*
◀ Artist: *Judas Priest* Lighting Designer: *Louis Ball* Year: *1986*

▲ Artist: *Genesis* Lighting Designer: *Marc Brickman* Year: *1992*

▲ Artist: *Yanni* Lighting Designer: *David 'Gurn' Kaniski* **Year:** *1991*

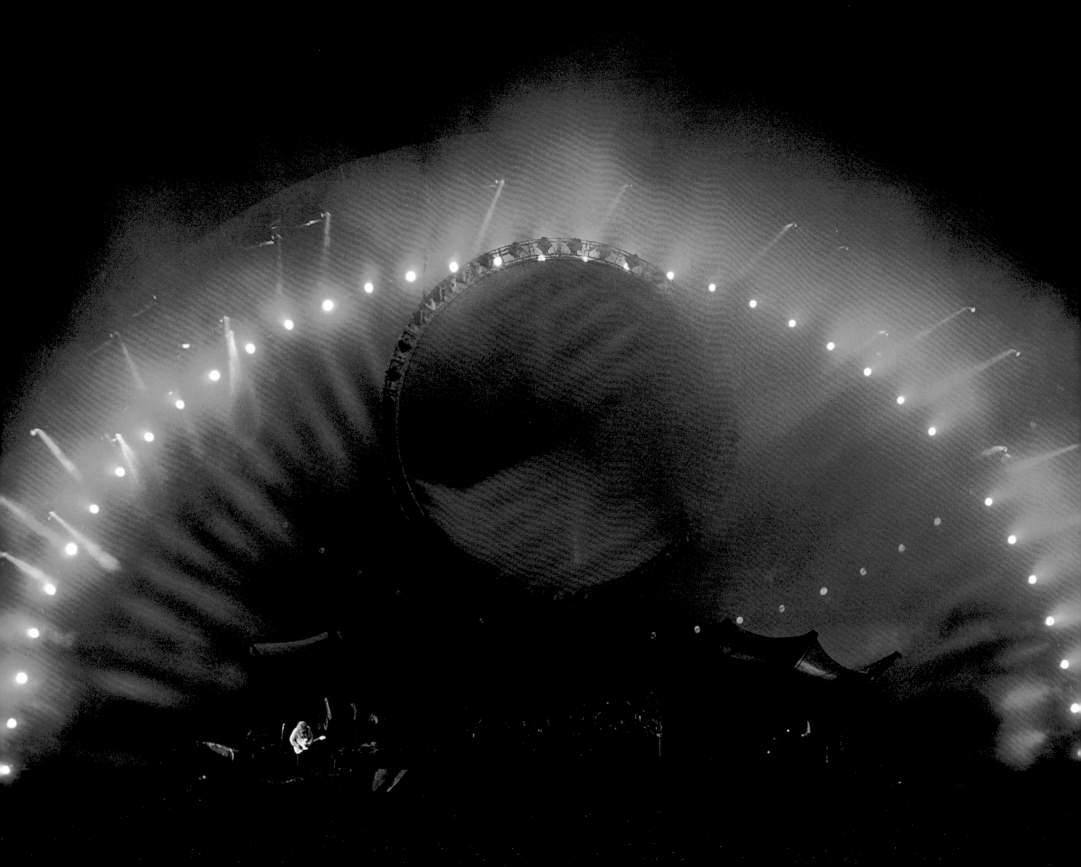

▲ Artist: *Barbara Mandrell* Lighting Designer: *Alan Owen* Year: *1993*
◀ Artist: *Pink Floyd* Lighting Designer: *Marc Brickman* Year: *1994*

Artist: *Genesis* Lighting Designer: *Alan Owen* Year: *1987* ▲
Artist: *Genesis* Lighting Designer: *Alan Owen* Year: *1983* ▶

▲ Artist: *Queensryche* Lighting Designer: *Howard Ungerleider* Year: *1991*

▲ Artist: *Bryan Adams* Lighting Designers: *LeRoy Bennett, John Featherstone* Year: *1992*

Artist: *The Cure* Lighting Designer: *LeRoy Bennett* Year: *1996* ▲
Artist: *Rush* Lighting Designer: *Howard Ungerleider* Year: *1992* ▶

▲ Artist: *Def Leppard* Year: *1993*

◀ Artist: *Tina Turner* Lighting Designer: *Patrick Woodroffe* Year: *1987*

Artist: *Cameo* Lighting Designer: *Alan Goldberg* Year: *1987* ▲
Artist: *Bon Jovi* Lighting Designer: *David Davidian* Year: *1989* ▶

▲ Artist: *Rush* Lighting Designer: *Howard Ungerleider* Year: *1988*

◀ Artist: *Kitaro* Lighting Designer: *Dale Polansky* Year: *1994*

Artist: *The Cure* Lighting Designer: *LeRoy Bennett* Year: *1992* ▲
Artist: *Depeche Mode* Lighting Designer: *Jane Spiers* Year: *1987* ▶

▲ Artist: *Genesis* Lighting Designer: *Marc Brickman* Year: *1992*

▲ Artist: *The Cure* Lighting Designer: *LeRoy Bennett* Year: *1992*

Artist: *Genesis* Lighting Designer: *Alan Owen* Year: *1987* ▲
Artist: *Rush* Lighting Designer: *Howard Ungerleider* Year: *1992* ▶

▲ Artist: *Dire Straits* Lighting Designer: *Chas Herington* Year: *1992*

▲ Event: *Tristan und Isolde* Designer: *David Hockney* Year: *1987*

Artist: *Genesis* Lighting Designer: *Marc Brickman* Year: *1992* ▲

Artist: *Genesis* Lighting Designer: *Alan Owen* Year: *1983* ▶

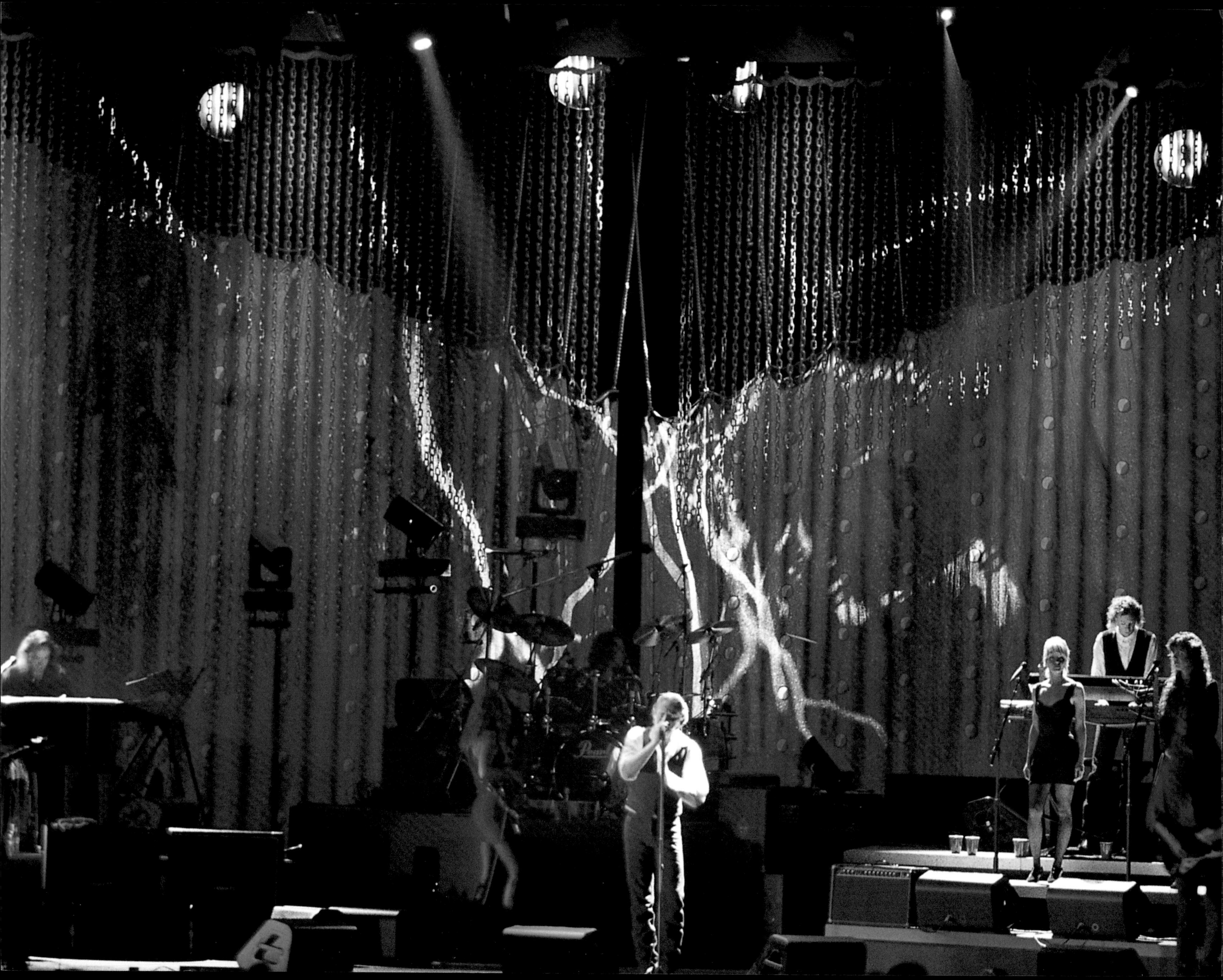

▲ Artist: *The Cure* Lighting Designer: *LeRoy Bennett* Year: *1989*
◀ Artist: *Don Henley* Lighting Designer: *Steve Cohen* Year: *1991*

▲ Artist: *Paul McCartney* Lighting Designer: *Marc Brickman* Year: *1993*

▲ Artist: *Amy Grant* Lighting Designer: *James Taylor* Year: *1995*

Artist: *Depeche Mode* Lighting Designer: *Jane Spiers* Year: *1987* ▲
Artist: *Pink Floyd* Lighting Designer: *Marc Brickman* Year: *1987* ▶

▲ Artist: *Rush* Lighting Designer: *Howard Ungerleider* Year: *1992*

▲ Artist: *Genesis* Lighting Designer: *Alan Owen* Year: *1983*

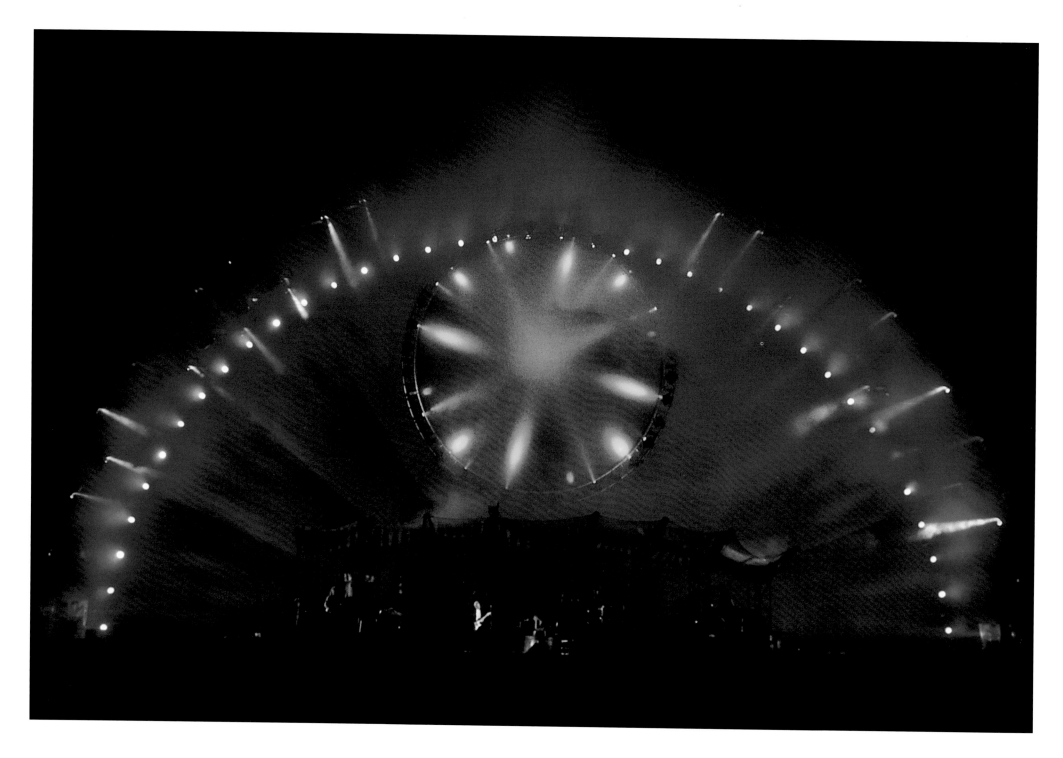

Artist: *Pink Floyd* Lighting Designer: *Marc Brickman* Year: *1994* ▲

▲ Artist: *George Michael* Lighting Designer: *LeRoy Bennett* Year: *1991*

▲ Artist: *Sarah McLachlan* Lighting Designer: *Graeme Nicol* Year: *1995*

▲ Artist: *Bon Jovi* Lighting Designer: *David Davidian* Year: *1993*

▲ Artist: *Sarah McLachlan* Lighting Designer: *Graeme Nicol* Year: *1995*

◄ Artist: *Depeche Mode* Lighting Designer: *LeRoy Bennett* Year: *1990*

Event: *The Magic Flute* Lighting Designer: *Richard Pilbrow* Year: *1993* ▲
Artist: *Mary Chapin Carpenter* Lighting Designer: *Allen Branton* Year: *1995* ▶

▲ Artist: *Elton John* Lighting Designer: *Steve Cohen* Year: *1992*

▲ Artist: *New Order* Lighting Designer: *Andy Liddle* Year: *1989*

▲ Artist: *Genesis* Lighting Designer: *Alan Owen* Year: *1987*

▲ Artist: *Genesis* Lighting Designer: *Alan Owen* Year: *1983*

▲ Artist: *Sarah McLachlan* Lighting Designer: *Graeme Nicol* Year: *1995*

◀ Artist: *Phil Collins* Lighting Designer: *Patrick Woodroffe* Year: *1994*

▲ Artist: *New Order* Lighting Designer: *Andy Liddle* Year: *1993*

▲ Artist: *Moody Blues* Lighting Designer: *Michael Keller* Year: *1991*

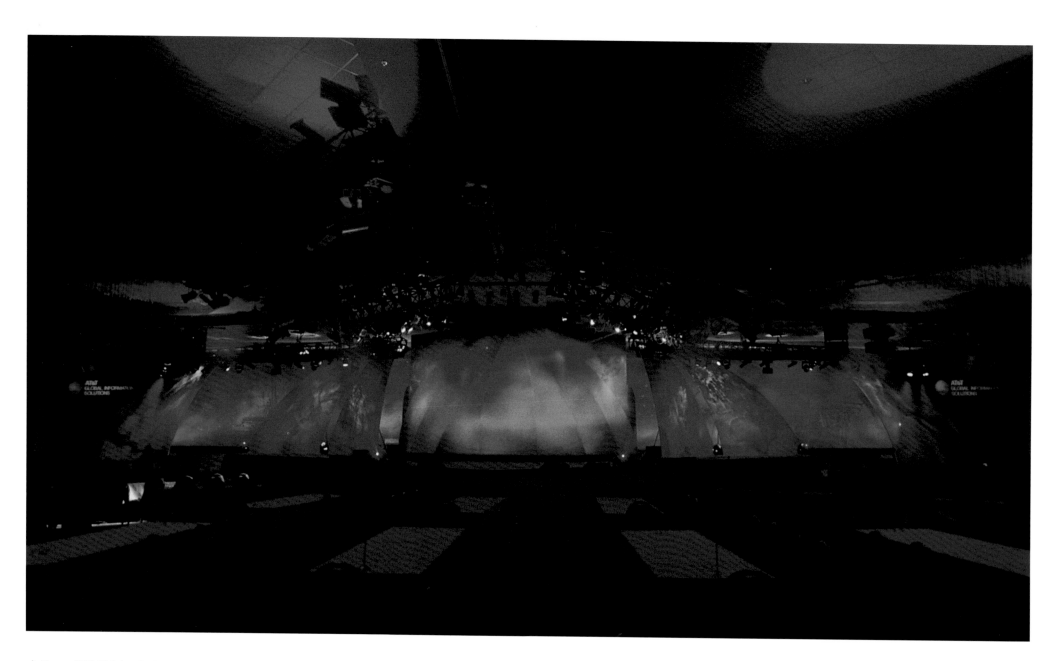

▲ Event: *AT&T* Lighting Designer: *Jay Gibson* Year: *1995*

▲ Artist: *BRING IN 'DA NOISE, BRING IN 'DA FUNK* Lighting Designers: *Jules Fisher, Peggy Eisenhauer* Year: *1996*

Artist: *Siegfried & Roy* Lighting Designer: *Andrew Bridge* Year: *1990 (Courtesy of Feld Entertainment)* ▲

Artist: *Genesis* Lighting Designer: *Marc Brickman* Year: *1992* ▶

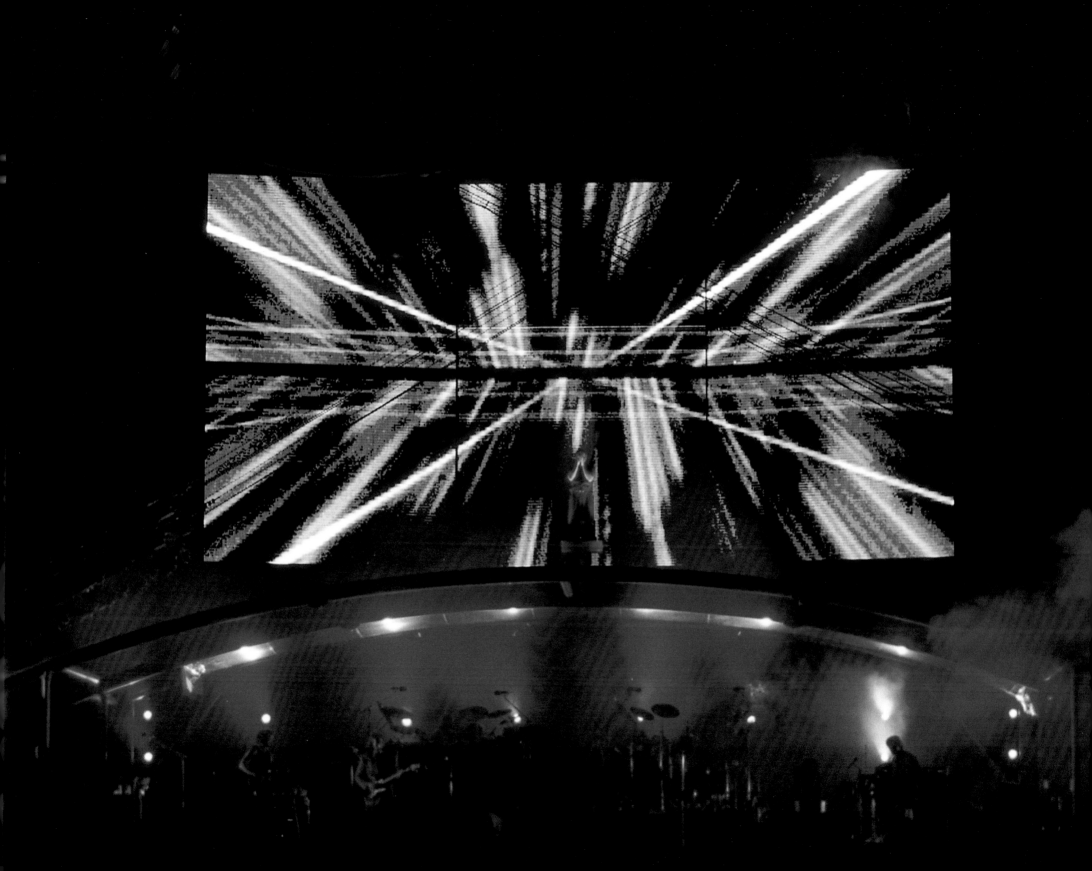

▲ Event: *The Who's 'Tommy'* Lighting Designer: *Chris Parry* Year: *1993*

◀ Artist: *The Judds* Lighting Designer: *Han Henzie* Year: *1990*

▲ Artist: *Janet Jackson* Lighting Designer: *LeRoy Bennett* Year: *1990*

▲ Artist: *Pink Floyd* Lighting Designer: *Marc Brickman* Year: *1994*

▲ Artist: *Dire Straits* Lighting Designer: *Chas Herington* Year: *1992*
◀ Artist: *Don Henley* Lighting Designer: *Steve Cohen* Year: *1990*

▲ Artist: *The Cure* Lighting Designer: *LeRoy Bennett* Year: *1996*

▲ Artist: *Yanni* Lighting Designer: *David 'Gurn' Kaniski* Year: *1993*

▲ Artist: *Sade* Lighting Designer: *LeRoy Bennett* Year: *1993*

▲ Artist: *New Order* Lighting Designer: *Andy Liddle* Year: *1993*

Artist: *Vince Gill* Lighting Designer: *Mike Swinford* Year: *1995* ▲
Artist: *New Order* Lighting Designer: *Andy Liddle* Year: *1993* ▶